Teaching Reading & Writing
With Favorite Songs

by Jacqueline Clarke

NEW YORK • TORONTO • LONDON • AUCKLAND • SYDNEY
MEXICO CITY • NEW DELHI • HONG KONG • BUENOS AIRES

Scholastic Inc. grants teachers permission to photocopy the reproducible pages from this book for classroom use. No other part of this publication may be reproduced in whole or in part, or stored in a retrieval system, or transmitted in any form or by any means, electronic, mechanical, photocopying, recording, or otherwise, without written permission of the publisher. For information regarding permission, write to Scholastic Teaching Resources, 557 Broadway, New York, NY 10012.

Cover design by Maria Lilja

Cover illustration by Martha Aviles

Interior design by Ellen Matlach Hassell
for Boultinghouse & Boultinghouse, Inc.

Interior illustrations by Maxie Chambliss

ISBN: 0-439-39512-7

Copyright © 2003 by Jacqueline Clarke.

Published by Scholastic Inc.

Printed in the U.S.A.

Contents

Introduction

When teaching children to read, we often start with what they know—letters in their name, environmental print, or words from a favorite book. Why not start with familiar songs? In this book, "Old MacDonald," "Wheels on the Bus," "This Old Man," and seven other favorites become springboards to lots of fun-filled learning. For each song, you'll find quick skill-building activities and appealing reproducibles that help children develop oral language, build phonemic awareness, expand their vocabularies, attend to print, and practice writing skills. Because song lyrics are repetitive and predictable, they are easy for children to learn. This oral familiarity then supports children when they encounter the lyrics in printed form. Teaching early literacy through music is not only effective, it's also a way to provide a joyful and community-building classroom experience for your students.

The activities for each song are divided into two sections: Develop Oral Language and Attend to Print. The first section includes activities for exploring the song orally. The second section describes reading and writing activities based on the written song lyrics. You'll find ideas on displaying and teaching with pocket charts, as well as reproducible collaborative class books and read-and-write mini-books. Listed below is an overview of the sections included for each song.

Develop Oral Language

Introduce the Song
This section describes a quick and easy way to introduce the song to children and spark their interest.

Sing It Again
Each day that you work with the song, begin by singing it aloud as a class. This section provides new ways to revisit the song and help children internalize its structure, lyrics, and tune.

Build Phonemic Awareness
Phonemic awareness is the understanding that words are made up of individual sounds (phonemes). The activities in this section help children build phonemic awareness through "playing" with various sounds from the song. The activities are broken down into the following tasks outlined by Wiley Blevins in *Phonemic Awareness Activities* (Scholastic, 1997):
- rhyme and alliteration
- oddity tasks
- oral blending
- oral segmentation
- phonemic manipulation

Attend to Print

Preparing the Pocket Chart

This section describes how to use a pocket chart to display all or some of the song lyrics. The next section, Read Together, outlines activities that invite children to interact with the pocket chart text in various ways.

Read Together

These activities are based on the lyrics displayed in the pocket chart and are similar to shared reading. They give children the opportunity to employ different reading strategies as they read the song, rather than sing it.

Write Together

In this section, you'll find a variety of writing activities: interactive writing, where students "share the pen" with the teacher; collaborative writing, where each child writes independently but contributes to a collective project; and individual writing, where each child adds writing to a mini-book that can be taken home and shared with families. All the writing projects are based on the song lyrics and reinforce what students have learned in previous sections.

A Weekly Plan

You might focus on one song each week, choosing a few activities every day. Once you've introduced the song, the rest of the activities can be used in any order. You can use all the activities and reproducibles for each song, or choose the ones that best meet the needs of your students and the requirements of your curriculum.

Here's a sample of a weekly plan:

Monday	Tuesday	Wednesday	Thursday	Friday
• Introduce the Song • Build Phonemic Awareness • Read Together	• Sing It Again • Build Phonemic Awareness • Read Together	• Sing It Again • Read Together • Write Together	• Sing It Again • Write Together	• Sing It Again • Write Together

How to Make the Mini-Books

Make single-sided copies of the mini-book pages. Fold each page in half horizontally and then vertically. If there are two pages in the book, nest one folded page inside the folded page with the cover on the front. Staple along the left-hand side. For young children, it is a good idea to assemble the mini-books ahead of time. Invite children to color the illustrations after they have added writing to the books.

Old MacDonald

Old MacDonald Had a Farm

Old MacDonald had a farm, E-I-E-I-O!
And on this farm he had a cow, E-I-E-I-O!
With a moo, moo here.
And a moo, moo there.
Here a moo, there a moo.
Everywhere a moo, moo.
Old MacDonald had a farm, E-I-E-I-O!

Additional Verses:

pig	oink, oink
sheep	baa, baa
horse	neigh, neigh
duck	quack, quack
cat	meow, meow

Develop Oral Language

Introduce the Song

Dress like Old MacDonald by wearing a straw hat, flannel shirt, and either overalls or jeans. Place the animal picture cards (page 8) in your pocket or hat. Use the cards to introduce each new verse by holding up the animals one at a time.

Sing It Again

- Ask each student to choose one animal from Old MacDonald's farm. Show them how to create a paper-plate mask of the animal. Attach craft sticks to the back of the masks to create handles. Invite students to wear their masks while singing the song. Instruct them to sing only their animal's part while you sing the remaining lines (for example, the student playing the part of the pig would sing "With an oink, oink here . . ."). Let students exchange masks and switch roles.

- To create stick puppets, draw a simple outline around the animal picture cards (page 8) and copy them onto heavy paper. Give each student a set of animals to cut out along the outline, color, and attach to craft sticks. Have children hold up the appropriate puppet and move it to the rhythm as you sing each verse together.

Build Phonemic Awareness

- **Oral Segmentation**   Draw an outline of a wide barn on a sheet of 8½- by 11-inch paper, and draw lines to divide it into three parts of approximately the same size. Give each child a photocopy of the barn and a marker (such as a chip or bean). Say each of the following words: *duck, cow, oink,* and *quack.* Have students listen for the /k/ sound and place a marker in one of the boxes to show its position in the word (beginning, middle, or end). Invite students to name other words that contain /k/ and identify the sound's position in each word.

- **Alliteration**   Work together with students to create silly alliterative sentences about Old MacDonald and the animals—for example, "Old MacDonald makes meatballs at midnight." You might have students illustrate their sentences and compile them into a class book.

- **Sound Discrimination**   Make a copy of the barn on page 9 and two sets of animal cards on page 8. Show students how to play "Who's in the Barn?" with a partner. Each player takes a set of cards. To take a turn, a player places one animal card under the barn (without showing the card) and gives a clue about the animal. For example, "This animal has the /ee/ sound in its name. Who's in the barn?" (*sheep*) If the other player guesses correctly, he or she earns 1 point. Players take turns until each player has earned 10 points.

Attend to Print

Preparing the Pocket Chart
Write the song title and each line of the first verse on sentence strips. Cut the strips into individual word cards. Then make word cards for the remaining animals and their sounds. Place the text for the first verse in the pocket chart. Copy, color, and cut apart the picture cards (pages 8–9) to display for each verse. Place the farmer and barn on each side of the song title.

Read Together
- Challenge students to read the text in different ways. For example, read only the first word in each line, the last word in each line, or every other word. Change the animal picture, name, and sound cards for each verse.

- Place the word *cow* in the pocket chart with the *oink* sound cards. Read the text again and wait for students to notice the error. Ask, "How do you know it doesn't say *moo*?" Continue to mix up animals and sounds and ask students to correct the errors.

- Remove all the cards from the pocket chart. Place either the animal name cards or picture cards in a column along the left-hand side of the pocket chart. Challenge students to place each sound card beside the appropriate animal card.

Write Together
- **Class Book**   Give each child a copy of the class book (page 10). Ask students to think of a birthday gift for Old MacDonald and to name the sound it makes—for example, popcorn and crunch. Show them how to write the name of the gift in the first blank and the sound word in the next eight blanks. Invite children to add an illustration. Add a cover and bind the pages together to form a class book titled "Happy Birthday, Old MacDonald!"

- **Banner**   Have students work together to draw a mother, father, and baby for several farm animals. Glue the families side by side onto a horizontal sheet of craft paper. Write the sentences shown at right under each family. Help children complete the blanks with the names of the female, male, and baby animal for each family (for example, cow, bull, calf; sow, boar, piglet; ewe, ram, lamb; hen, rooster, chick).

| **Animal Names** |
| My mother is a _____. |
| My father is a _____. |
| I am a _____. |

- **Mini-Book**   Give each child a copy of the mini-book (pages 11–12). Have students write their name on the cover. Read the text with them and help them fill in the blanks with animal names and sounds.

Picture Cards

Picture Cards

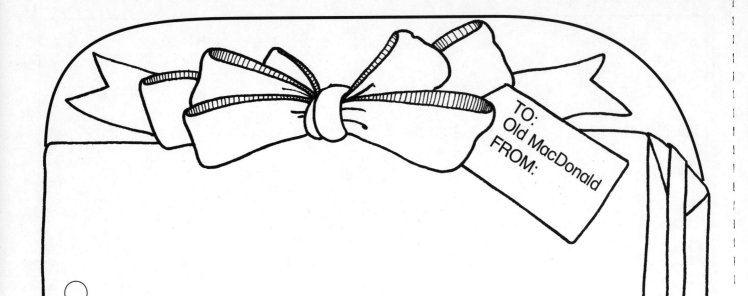

To:
Old MacDonald
FROM:

Old MacDonald had a birthday, E-I-E-I-O!

And on his birthday he got a

_____, E-I-E-I-O!

With a _____, _____ here.

And a _____, _____ there.

Here a _____, there a _____.

Everywhere a _____, _____.

Old MacDonald had a birthday, E-I-E-I-O!

Name _____

Teaching Reading & Writing With Favorite Songs   Scholastic Teaching Resources

Class Book

Old MacDonald

had a _____.

Here a quack, there a quack.

Everywhere a _____,

_____.

Old MacDonald had a farm.

E-I-E-I-O.

Old MacDonald

Name _____

Old MacDonald

had a _____.

Here a meow, there a meow.

Everywhere a _____,

_____.

Old MacDonald

had a _____ .

Here a baa, there a baa.

Everywhere a _____ ,

_____ .

Old MacDonald

had a _____ .

Here an oink, there an oink.

Everywhere an _____ ,

_____ .

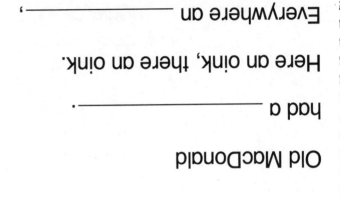

Old MacDonald

had a _____ .

Here a neigh, there a neigh.

Everywhere a _____ ,

_____ .

Old MacDonald

had a _____ .

Here a moo, there a moo.

Everywhere a _____ ,

_____ .

Mary Wore Her Red Dress

VOCABULARY

- Clothing Names
- Color Words

Mary Wore Her Red Dress

Mary wore her red dress,
red dress, red dress.
Mary wore her red dress
all day long.

Additional Verses:

Sam	orange sweater
Hannah	pink sneakers
Peter	blue jeans
Leon	green shirt
Ashley	yellow hat

Develop Oral Language

Introduce the Song

Gather articles of clothing to match the ones mentioned in the song (or enlarge the picture cards on page 15 and color them accordingly). Place the clothes or picture cards in a suitcase. As you sing each verse, pull out the appropriate article of clothing and hold it up for students to see. After singing all the verses, ask children to look at their own clothing. How many are wearing clothes that are similar to those named in the song?

If you are unfamiliar with this song, refer to the picture book and audio tape *Mary Wore Her Red Dress and Henry Wore His Green Sneakers* by Merle Peek (Clarion, 1993).

Sing It Again

- Add a new twist to the song. Copy and cut apart the picture cards, then color them so that they do not match the song lyrics. Hold up the appropriate card before you sing each verse and sing the song using the new colors, such as "Mary wore her purple dress."

- Substitute *Mary* and *red dress* with students' names and articles of clothing (such as "Al wore his orange vest"). Repeat until all students have had a turn.

Build Phonemic Awareness

- **Oral Blending** Say each color word slowly to emphasize each part, such as /r/ /e/ /d/. Ask children to listen carefully and then name the word as a whole. Repeat the activity using clothing words and students' names.

- **Oddity Task** Read the following sets of clothing words aloud. Ask students to name the word in each set that doesn't begin with the same initial sound:

  pants, pajamas, hat
  sandals, coat, socks
  belt, shirt, shoes

Attend to Print

Preparing the Pocket Chart

Create a sentence strip for each child mentioned in the song following this pattern: "Mary wore her red dress," "Sam wore his orange sweater," and so on. Cut the strips into individual word cards. Place the text in the pocket chart. Cut out a paper square to match each color mentioned in the song. Copy, color, and cut apart the picture cards (page 15) to use in the activities.

Read Together

- Let students take turns matching the clothing picture cards and colored squares to the appropriate words in the text.

- Ask questions such as "Who wore a red dress?" or "What color were Hannah's sneakers?" Invite children to point to the words in the text that answer the questions (for example, *Mary*, *pink*).

- Mix up the names in the text. Challenge students to put them back in the correct order. Encourage them to use the words *his* and *her* as clues.

- Remove the word cards for "Mary wore her red dress" and give each card to a different student. Challenge the five students to rebuild the sentence by arranging themselves in the correct order. Repeat using other lines from the song until everyone has had a turn.

Write Together

- **Class Book**   Give each child a copy of the class book page (page 16). Read the text aloud and explain that children should fill in a name in the first blank, a color word in the second, and an article of clothing in the third. Tell children that they might write about themselves or a made-up character. Invite them to draw an illustration to match what they have written. Add a cover and staple the pages together to form a class book.

- **Catalog**   Ask children to cut out pictures of different articles of clothing from magazines or catalogs, or draw and cut out small pictures of their own. Work together with children to sort the clothing into categories (pants, jackets, sweaters, hats, and so on). On 11- by 17-inch sheets of construction paper, draw a large outline of each type of clothing and glue the pictures inside. Work with children to create labels for the different categories. Staple the pages together and add a decorative cover. Share the "catalog" with children and ask them to tell you which items they like the most and least. For a math activity, add prices to the items and have students pretend to shop for clothes. Determine an amount of money that each child can spend.

- **Mini-Book**   Give each child a copy of the mini-book (pages 17–18). Have children write their name on the cover. Read the text with them and help them fill in the blanks with the appropriate color and clothing words. On the last page, instruct children to illustrate the text with a picture of themselves.

Picture Cards

_____ wore

a _____ _____

all day long.

Teaching Reading & Writing With Favorite Songs Scholastic Teaching Resources

Name _____

7

all day long.

_____ _____

Ashley wore her
yellow hat, yellow hat.
Ashley wore her yellow hat,

2

all day long.

_____ _____

Mary wore her
red dress, red dress.
Mary wore her red dress,

I wore my _____

_____.

all day long.

8

Mary Wore Her Red Dress

Name _____

1

all day long.

_____ _____

Peter wore his

Peter wore his blue jeans,
blue jeans, blue jeans.

all day long.

_____ _____

Hannah wore her

Hannah wore her pink sneakers,
pink sneakers, pink sneakers.

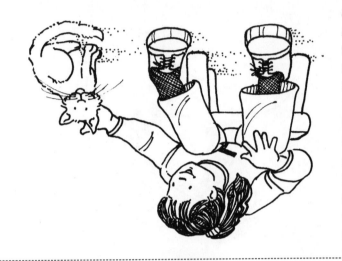

Leon wore his green shirt,
green shirt, green shirt.

Leon wore his

_____ _____

all day long.

Sam wore his orange sweater,
orange sweater, orange sweater.

Sam wore his

_____ _____

all day long.

Five Green and Speckled Frogs

Five Green and Speckled Frogs

Five green and speckled frogs
sat on a speckled log,
eating some most delicious bugs.
YUM! YUM!
One jumped into the pool
where it was nice and cool.
Then there were four green speckled frogs.
GLUB! GLUB!

Additional Verses:

Four	Then there were three . . .
Three	Then there were two . . .
Two	Then there was one . . .
One	Then there were no . . .

Develop Oral Language

Introduce the Song

Draw five frogs on the chalkboard. Erase a frog each time you sing "One jumped into the pool." Ask students, "Is this song an adding song or a subtracting song? How do you know?"

If you are unfamiliar with this song, refer to the *Ultimate Kids Song Collection*, which includes 101 favorite songs on CD (Madacy Records, 2000). Search for this song collection on www.amazon.com to listen to the tune of "Five Green and Speckled Frogs."

Sing It Again

• Create five frog masks from paper plates. Attach a craft stick to the back of each. Let children take turns wearing the masks and acting out the song as you sing the song together.

• Make copies of the finger puppets on page 21 so that you have five for each student. Have students color and cut out the frogs. Help them tape the bands together to fit their fingers. Instruct students to wear all five puppets on one hand. As you sing together, have students remove one puppet each time you sing about a frog jumping into the pool.

Build Phonemic Awareness

• **Alliteration**   Work together with students to create silly alliterative sentences about the five frogs in the song. For example, "Five frogs feasted on french fries at the farm." Let students illustrate the sentences and compile the pages into a class book.

• **Oral Segmentation**   Slowly say a word from the song, such as *green*, exaggerating each sound in the word. Then ask students to hop like a frog for each sound they heard. With each hop, have them say the sound of the phoneme.

Attend to Print

Preparing the Pocket Chart

Write the song lyrics for the first verse on sentence strips, leaving spaces for the words *five* and *four*. Place the text in the pocket chart. Make two sets of cards for several color words. Cut colored construction paper to create cards that are the same colors as the words. Then make cards for number words and numerals from 1 to 5 (or 1 to 10 for additional practice).

Read Together

- Insert the 5 card in the first blank and the 4 card in the second blank. Place all the number words at the bottom of the pocket chart. Read the song lyrics together. Ask a volunteer to match the number words with the appropriate numerals. Repeat with other numerals and number words.

- Make a frog pointer using one of the finger puppets (page 21) and a dowel. Ask students to use the pointer to find words in the text that contain the short-*o* sound. Repeat the activity with other short and long vowels.

- Replace the word *green* with a different color word card. Ask students to read the text with the new color. Repeat with other color words.

- Remove all cards from the pocket chart. Place the color cards in a column along the left-hand side. Challenge students to place each color word card beside the appropriate color card.

Write Together

- **Class Book**   Divide the class into groups of five. Assign each child in a group a different number, from 1 to 5. Give each child a copy of the class book (page 22). Explain that they should write their number word in the first blank and a color word in the second. (If their number word is *one*, cross out or cover up the *s* in *frogs*.) Ask students to think of something silly that the frogs could be eating, such as ice cream or bananas. Have them draw and color an illustration to match the text. Invite each group to create a cover and make up a title, such as "Frog Count." Staple each group's pages in numerical order.

- **Silly Story**   Write the following on sentence strips:

      Today I went for a walk and I saw
      one green speckled frog,
      two red _____ _____,
      three orange _____ _____,

  and so on. Place the strips in the pocket chart. Work together with students to create word cards for adjectives (*striped, spotted, freckled, polka-dotted, plaid*) and animals (*cows, pigs, sheep*). On each line, place an adjective card in the first blank and an animal card in the second blank. Read the story aloud together. Invite students to rearrange the word cards to create new stories.

- **Mini-Book**   Give each child a copy of the mini-book on page 23. Have students write their name on the cover. Read the text with them and help them fill in the blanks on page 2 with the words *five* and *green*. Instruct them to write the word *green* on page 4. Invite students to color the pages.

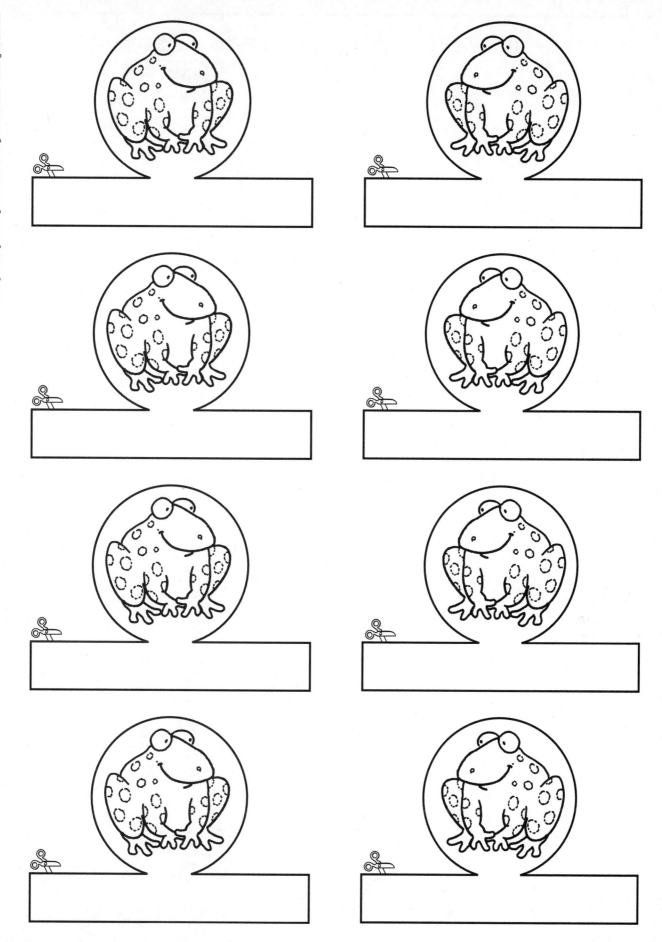

Finger Puppets

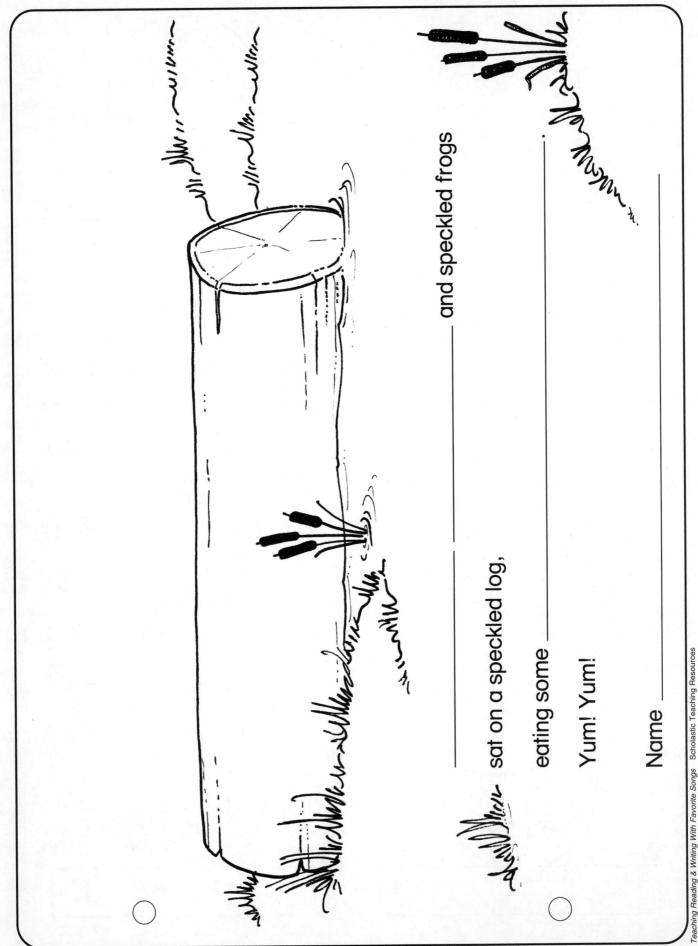

and speckled frogs

_____

sat on a speckled log,

eating some _____

Yum! Yum!

Name _____

Teaching Reading & Writing With Favorite Songs Scholastic Teaching Resources

Class Book

They jumped into the pool
where it was nice and cool.

YUM! YUM!
eating some most delicious bugs.
sat on a speckled log,
and speckled frogs
_____

Then there were no _____
speckled frogs.
GLUB! GLUB!

Five Green and Speckled Frogs

Name _____

Wheels on the Bus

Wheels on the Bus

The wheels on the bus go round and round,
round and round, round and round.
The wheels on the bus go round and round,
all through the town.

Additional Verses:

wipers	swish, swish, swish	(Bend arms, move from right to left.)
horn	beep, beep, beep	(Press palm of hand on imaginary horn.)
seats	squeak, squeak, squeak	(Move hips from right to left.)
babies	waa, waa, waa	(Move fists in front of face, as if rubbing eyes.)
parents	sh, sh, sh	(Put finger to lips in a whisper.)

Develop Oral Language

Introduce the Song

Teach children the motions for each verse of the song. Show them how to do each motion quickly as they sing the repeated sound words. Then sing the song together with everyone moving to the rhythm.

Sing It Again

- Make several copies of the picture cards (page 26) and give one to each student. Explain that students should listen for their word in the song. When they hear it, they should hold their card high in the air. Let children trade cards and repeat the activity.

- Arrange chairs in rows of four with an "aisle" between each pair of chairs to resemble a school bus. Choose one child to be the driver and sit in a chair in the front. Have the rest of the children find seats on the "bus." Instruct the driver to lead the group in singing the song as he or she pretends to drive the bus.

- Invite children to create additional verses about other objects or people found on the bus—for example, "The brakes on the bus go screech, screech, screech." Sing the new verses together.

Build Phonemic Awareness

- **Alliteration**   Choose a letter sound such as /k/. Say, "I'm going on a bus trip and I'm going to bring a carrot." Ask the next child to repeat your sentence and add another word that begins with the same sound. Continue until everyone has had a turn. Repeat with other sounds.

- **Oral Segmentation**   On a sheet of 8½- by 11-inch paper, draw a large simple outline of a bus and draw lines to divide it into three equal sections. Give each student a photocopy of the sheet and three markers (such as beans or chips). Say the word *bus*. Ask students where they hear the /b/ sound—at the beginning, middle, or end of the word. Show them how to place a counter in the front of the bus to show that they hear the sound at the beginning of the word. Repeat with other /b/ words.

Attend to Print

Preparing the Pocket Chart

Create a sentence strip for each verse of the song following this pattern: "The wheels on the bus go round and round," "The wipers on the bus go swish, swish, swish," and so on. Cut the strips into individual word cards. Place the text in the pocket chart. Copy, color, and cut apart the picture cards (page 26).

Read Together

- Hold up a picture card. Ask a volunteer to point to the word in the text that matches the picture. Repeat with other pictures.

- Point to one set of sound words in the song, such as *swish, swish, swish*. Ask children to do the motion that matches the words (see page 24). Repeat with other sound words. Reverse the activity by doing the motion and having students point to the matching words in the text.

- Write *bus* on the chalkboard. Ask children to change one letter to create another word. (You might give them the word to create, such as *bun*.) Repeat with other words. For example:

  go–add one letter to spell *got*   horn–change one letter to spell *torn*

Write Together

- **Class Book**   Give each child a copy of the class book (page 27). Have students choose an object with wheels, such as a bike, skateboard, or tractor. Then challenge them to think of the sound it might make. Show them how to write the name of object in the first blank (*bike*) and the sound word in the next three (*whir, whir, whir*). Invite children to illustrate the page to match the text. Add a cover with the title "Wheels All Around" and staple the pages together to form a class book.

- **Poetry**   On two separate sentence strips, write, "Listen, listen, listen" and "A classroom full of sounds!" Place the first strip at the top of the pocket chart and the second at the bottom. Give each child a sentence strip with the following frame: The _____ go _____. Have students choose an object from the classroom and think of the sound that it makes. Show children how to write the name of the object in the first blank and the sound it makes in the second. (If the object is singular, have them add *es* to the word *go*.) Have a few children at a time place their sentence strips in the pocket chart between the sentences. Invite children to read the poem aloud with you. Then remove students' strips and add other students' sentences.

- **Mini-Book**   Give each child a copy of the mini-book (pages 28–29). Have students write their name on the cover. Read the text with them and help them fill in the blanks with the missing words.

Picture Cards

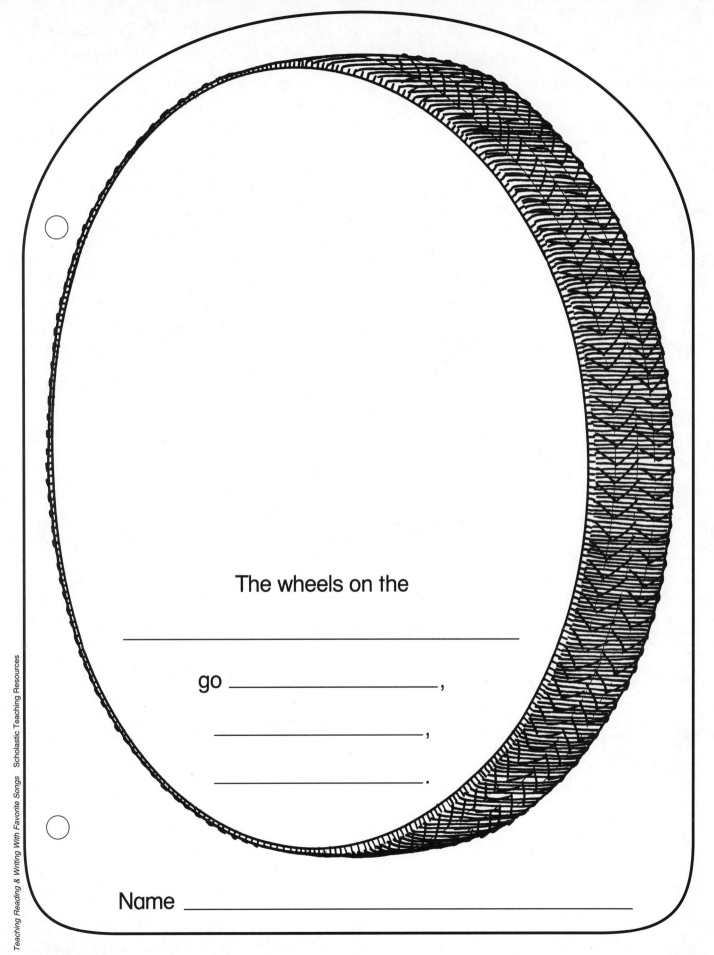

The wheels on the

_____

go _____ ,

_____ ,

_____ .

Name _____

The _____
on the bus
go sh, sh, sh.

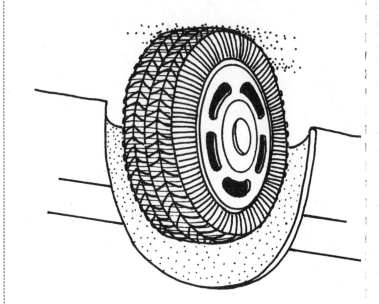

The _____
on the bus
go round and round.

. . . all through the town.

8

Wheels on the Bus

Name _____

1

The _____
on the bus
go squeak, squeak, squeak.

The _____
on the bus
goes beep, beep, beep.

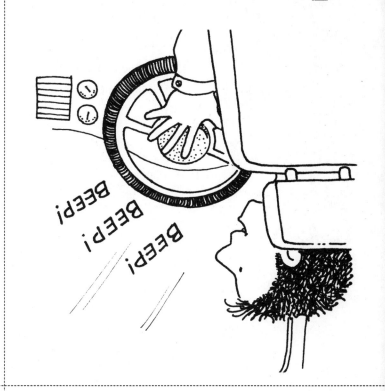

The _____
on the bus
go waa, waa, waa.

The _____
on the bus
go swish, swish, swish.

28 MAIN ST.

35

Who Stole the Cookies?

Who Stole the Cookies?

Who stole the cookies from the cookie jar?
_____ stole the cookies from the cookie jar.
Who, me?
Yes, you.
Couldn't be!
Then who?

Develop Oral Language

Introduce the Song

Make enough copies of the cookie cards (page 32) so that you have one for every student. Cut out the cookies and label each one with a student's name. Place the cookies in a container. Remove a cookie from the "cookie jar" and sing that child's name in the second line. Ask that child to sing "Who me?" and "Couldn't be!" Repeat with other children's names until everyone has had a turn. After singing the first verse, skip the first line of the song.

Sing It Again

- Have children sit in a circle on the floor. Invite them to clap to the rhythm as you sing the song again. Toss a beanbag or a soft ball to the student whose name will be used in the song. For the next verse, ask the student to toss the beanbag to someone else and sing the song again with that child's name. Explain that children should toss the beanbag to someone who has not yet had a turn.

- Sing the song in the same manner as described above, but use different voices for each verse. Whisper, sing in high voices, sing in low voices, and so on. Or you might ask children to sing like a giant, a monster, a robot, or an opera singer.

Build Phonemic Awareness

- **Phonemic Manipulation**   Challenge students to substitute the first sound in their name with a different sound, such as /g/. Sing the song using students' altered names—for example, *Kate* would be *Gate*. Repeat with other sounds.

- **Oral Segmentation**   Give each child a cookie card (page 32) and a few chocolate chips (or nonedible manipulatives, such as dried beans). Say a student's name. Ask children to count the number of sounds they hear in the name and place that number of chocolate chips on the cookie. Repeat with other children's names. You might allow students to eat the chocolate chips when you are finished with the activity. Check with families about food allergies and dietary restrictions first.

Attend to Print

Preparing the Pocket Chart

Write the song lyrics on sentence strips, leaving a blank as shown in the lyrics on page 30. Cut the strips into individual words. Place the text in the pocket chart. Write each student's name on a word card.

Read Together

- Insert a student's name in the blank space. Cover up the name with a blank card. Move the card slowly to reveal one letter at a time until students correctly guess the name.

- Create a second set of word cards of the song lyrics. Hand out one word card to each student. Invite students to match their word to one in the pocket chart. Have students switch cards and repeat.

- Cover a word with a cookie card (use more than one if necessary). Ask students to read the text and figure out the hidden word. Repeat with different words.

- Point out the three types of punctuation marks in the song lyrics (question mark, period, exclamation point). Read the lyrics, emphasizing how each type of punctuation affects the way a sentence is read. Provide other examples and have children read them aloud together.

Write Together

- **Class Book**   Write the names of well-known storybook characters on index cards (Corduroy, Paddington, Miss Spider, and so on). Place the cards in a bag and let each child choose one. Give each child a copy of the class book on page 33. Instruct them to fill in the blank line with the name they selected and then illustrate the page to match the text. Or ask children to think of a character they would like to write about and draw. Add a cover and bind the pages together to form a class book.

- **Word Bank/Chant**   Work together with children to create a word bank of different types of cookies (oatmeal, chocolate chip, and so on). Teach children the following chant, filling in the blanks with a type of cookie from the word bank.

    I like cookies.
    I like cookies.

    _____, _____
    I like cookies!

- **Mini-Book**   Give each child a copy of the mini-book (pages 34–35). Have them write their name on the front cover. Read the text with them. On the last page, have children write which character from the mini-book they think stole the cookies. Invite them to draw a picture to illustrate their guess. Encourage students to read the books with a classmate before bringing them home to share with families.

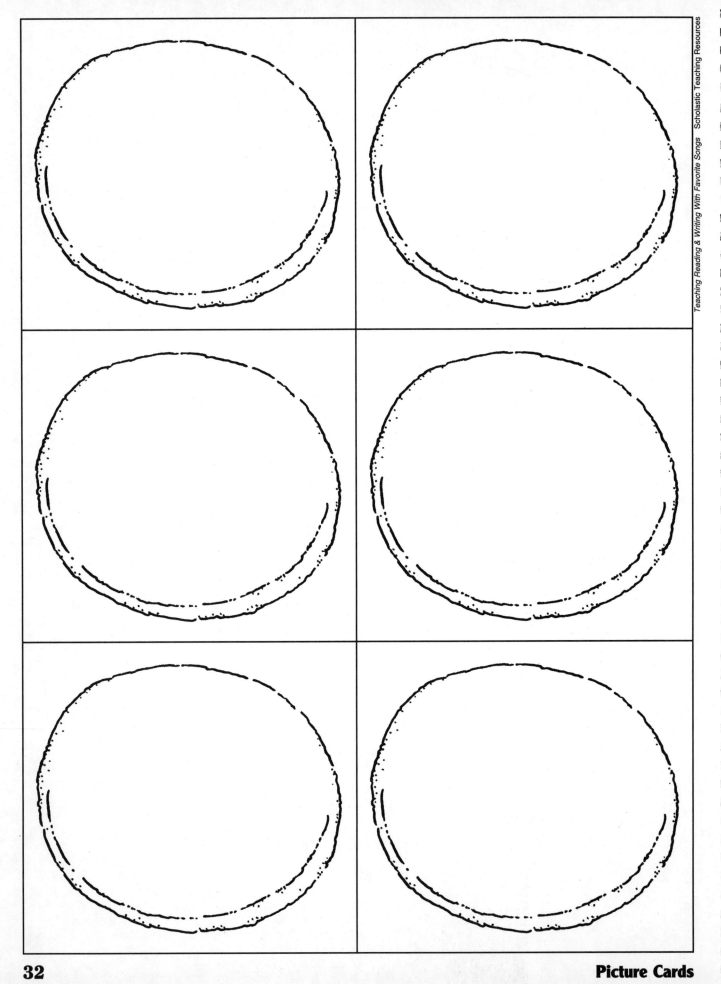

Teaching Reading & Writing With Favorite Songs   Scholastic Teaching Resources

Picture Cards

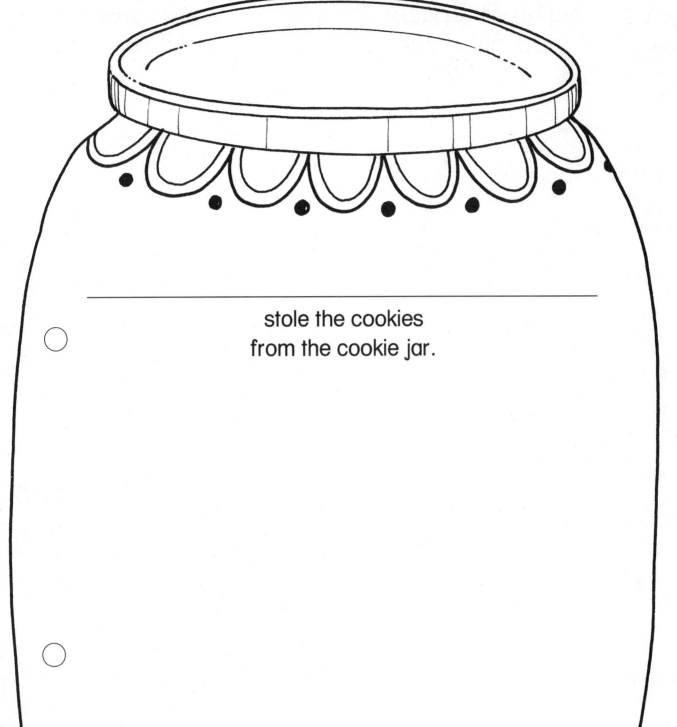

stole the cookies
from the cookie jar.

Name _____

Jack Horner stole the cookies
from the cookie jar.
Who me? Couldn't be!

Who stole the cookies
from the cookie jar?

Who do you think stole the
cookies?

_____

Draw a picture here.

Who Stole
the Cookies?

Name _____

Mother Goose stole the cookies
from the cookie jar.
Who me? Couldn't be!

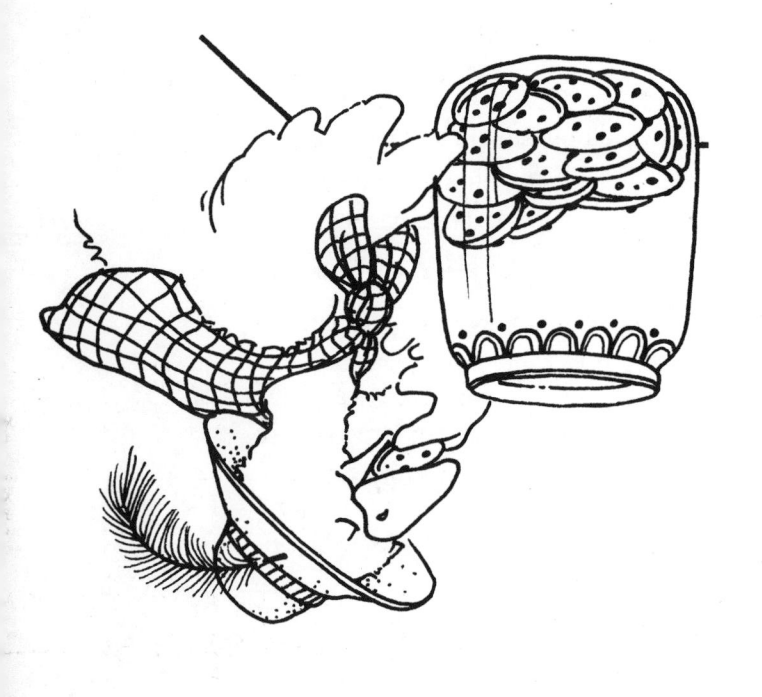

Miss Muffet stole the cookies
from the cookie jar.
Who me? Couldn't be!

Humpty Dumpty stole the cookies
from the cookie jar.
Who me? Couldn't be!

Bo Peep stole the cookies
from the cookie jar.
Who me? Couldn't be!

This Old Man

This Old Man

This old man,	(Place hands on hips.)
he played one.	(Hold up one finger.)
He played knick-knack on my thumb.	(Point to thumb.)
With a knick-	(Pat right thigh with right hand.)
knack	(Pat left thigh with left hand.)
paddy-	(Pat left shoulder with right hand.)
whack,	(Pat right shoulder with left hand.)
give a dog a bone.	(Place hands palms up.)
This old man came rolling	(Roll hands over each other.)
home!	(Point thumbs over shoulders.)

Additional Verses:

two—on my shoe	(Hold up two fingers; point to shoe.)
three—on my knee	(Hold up three fingers; tap knee.)
four—on my door	(Hold up four fingers; make knocking motion.)
five—on my hive	(Hold up five fingers; tap fist.)
six—on my sticks	(Hold up six fingers; tap pointer fingers together.)

Develop Oral Language

Introduce the Song

Enlarge the picture cards (page 38), color them, and cut them apart. Paste each one onto a 5- by 8-inch index card. Write the corresponding number for each picture on the back of the index card. Place the cards in numerical order on the chalkboard ledge. As you sing each verse, turn the card over to reveal the picture.

Sing It Again

• Teach children the motions to the song. Invite them to use the motions as you sing the song together.

• Place the picture/number cards (see Introduce the Song) on the chalkboard ledge arranged from 6 to 1. Sing the song in this order to reinforce counting backward.

Build Phonemic Awareness

• **Phonemic Manipulation**   Choose a letter sound such as /t/ and challenge students to substitute the initial consonants in *knick-knack paddy-whack* with that sound (*tick-tack taddy-tack*). Sing the song together with this new twist, then repeat with other letter sounds.

- **Rhyme**   Copy and cut apart the picture cards (page 38). Write the numerals 1 to 6 on 3- by 5-inch index cards. Pass out both the picture cards and number cards to students. Challenge them to find a classmate whose card has a picture or number that rhymes with their own. Repeat until all students have had a turn. Read the rhymes aloud. Explain that *one* and *thumb* sound alike but do not rhyme.

Attend to Print

Preparing the Pocket Chart

Write the lyrics for the first verse on sentence strips, leaving blanks: *This old man, he played _____. He played knick-knack on my _____.* Cut the strips into individual words. Place the text in the pocket chart. Copy, color, and cut apart the picture cards (page 38). Create a set of word cards to match the picture cards, as well as numeral cards and number word cards for 1–6.

Read Together

- Place all the number word cards and picture word cards at the bottom of the pocket chart. Place the cards for the numeral 1 and the picture of the thumb in the blank spaces. Read the text aloud. Challenge students to find the words *one* and *thumb* and place them over the matching numeral or picture in the text. Repeat with other numerals and pictures.

- Place either a numeral or number word card in the first blank. Leave the second blank empty. Hand out the picture cards to several students. Read the text aloud. Explain that the student holding the matching picture card should place it in the second blank (for example, *five* and *hive*). Repeat with other numbers.

- Point to a word in the pocket chart, such as *man*. Challenge students to find another word that is similar in at least one way. For example, *man* and *knack* both have the short *a* sound in them and *man* and *dog* have the same number of letters. Repeat with other words.

- Remove all the cards from the pocket chart. Place the numeral cards in a column along the left-hand side of the pocket chart. Hand out the number word cards and let students match them to the numerals. Repeat the activity using the picture cards and picture words.

Write Together

- **Class Book**   Give each student a copy of the class book (page 39). Assign each student a different letter. Ask students to write their letter in the first blank and a word beginning with that letter in the second. Let them illustrate the page to match the text. Staple the pages together to create a class book.

- **Poetry**   Create rhyming couplets using number words. Write "One, one" on chart paper. Work together with children to create a phrase or sentence that rhymes with the number. For example, "One, one, school is fun." Repeat with other numbers ("Two, two, the sky is blue" or "Three, three, climb a tree").

- **Mini-Book**   Give each child a copy of the mini-book (pages 40–41). Have students write their name on the cover. Read the text with them and help them fill in the blanks with number words. Encourage them to read their book with a classmate before bringing it home to share with families.

Picture Cards

A B C D E F G H I J K L M

This old man, he played _____.

He played knick-knack on my _____.

With a knick-knack paddy-whack,
give a dog a bone.
This old man came rolling home!

N O P Q R S T U V W X Y Z

Name _____

This old man,

he played ——————.

He played knick-knack
on my sticks.

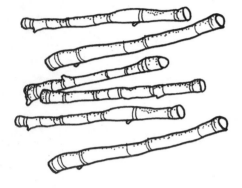

7

This old man,

he played ——————.

He played knick-knack
on my thumb.

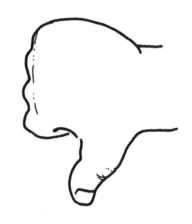

2

With a knick-knack
paddy-whack,
give a dog a bone.
This old man came
rolling home!

8

This Old Man

Name _____

1

He played knick-knack
on my door.

he played ————.

This old man,

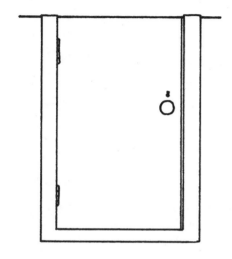

4

He played knick-knack
on my knee.

he played ————.

This old man,

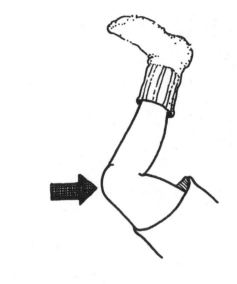

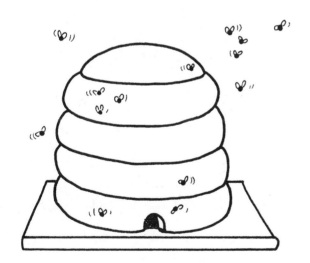

This old man,

he played ————————.

He played knick-knack
on my hive.

This old man,

he played ————————.

He played knick-knack
on my shoe.

If You're Happy and You Know It

VOCABULARY

■ **Action Words**

■ **Feeling Words**

If You're Happy and You Know It

If you're happy and you know it, clap your hands.
If you're happy and you know it, clap your hands.
If you're happy and you know it,
then your face will surely show it.
If you're happy and you know it, clap your hands.

Additional Verses:
stomp your feet
wiggle your toes
blink your eyes
touch your nose
shout *Hooray!*

Develop Oral Language

Introduce the Song

Play Simon Says to teach children the motions in the song lyrics. Give instructions such as, "Simon says touch your nose. Simon says blink your eyes. Clap your hands." After the game, sing the song together with everyone doing the motions.

Sing It Again

• Add a verse at the end of the song that begins: "If you're happy and you know it, do all six." Then challenge children to do all six motions in the order they appear in the song, without naming them.

• Copy, color, and cut apart the picture cards (page 44). On 3- by 5-inch index cards, write each of the verbs used in the song (*clap, stomp, wiggle, blink, touch,* and *shout*). Place the picture cards in one paper bag and the verb cards in another. Let students take turns choosing one card from each bag. Sing the song together using these new words—for example, "If you're happy and you know it, blink your feet." Challenge students to make up a motion for each new verse.

Build Phonemic Awareness

• **Oral Segmentation**   Say a word from the song, such as *happy*. Ask children to clap (or stomp, blink, and so on) once for each syllable. Continue with different words and actions from the song.

• **Sound Discrimination**   Ask students to listen carefully and act accordingly as you sing the following adaptation of the song:

> If your name begins with *T*, clap your hands.
> If your name begins with *T* clap your hands.
> If your name begins with *T*, you should listen carefully,
> If your name begins with *T*, clap your hands.

Repeat with other letters until all students have had a chance to clap.

Attend to Print

Preparing the Pocket Chart

Write the first sentence of each verse on sentence strips. ("If you're happy and you know it, clap your hands. If you're happy and you know it, stomp your feet," and so on.) Cut the strips into individual word cards. Place the text in the pocket chart. Copy, color, and cut apart the picture cards (page 44). Create word cards for each of the following adjectives: *angry, sad, scared, proud, excited,* and *silly*.

Read Together

- Let students take turns matching the picture cards to the words in the text. Then reverse the activity. Display the picture cards instead of the word cards. Have students match the words to the pictures.

- Rearrange the words in the text that name parts of the body. Invite children to read the text aloud. Challenge them to put the words back in the correct order.

- Point to a verb in the text, such as *wiggle* or *blink*. Challenge students to read the word and do the action. Repeat with other verbs.

- Substitute the word *happy* each time it appears with the six adjective cards. Challenge students to read the new adjectives and then read each line aloud together. Invite students to do the motions for those verses.

Write Together

- **Class Book** Give each student a copy of the class book page (page 45). Have them fill in the first blank with a feeling word, such as *joyful* or *nervous*, the second with an action word, and the third with a part of the body. Let them illustrate the face to match the feeling word. Add a cover and bind the pages together to create a class book.

- **Poster** Brainstorm a list of feeling words with children. Work together to write the words along the left-hand side of a sheet of chart paper. Have students draw faces to illustrate the words. Paste the faces on the right-hand side of the chart next to the corresponding feeling word. Display the poster in your classroom and let children use it as a resource when you ask, "How are you feeling today?"

- **Mini-Book** Give each child a copy of the mini-book (pages 46–47). Have students write their name on the cover. Read the text with them and help them fill in the blanks with names of body parts, such as hands or feet. Remind students to use the illustrations as clues to help them figure out the missing words. Encourage them to read their book with a classmate before bringing it home to share with families.

Picture Cards

If you're _____ and you know it,

_____ your _____.

Name _____

Teaching Reading & Writing With Favorite Songs   Scholastic Teaching Resources

7

touch your _____,

2

If you're happy and you know it

If You're Happy and You Know It

Name _____

1

shout *Hooray!*

8

5 wiggle your _____,

4 stomp your _____,

blink your _____,

clap your _____,

3

Teaching Reading & Writing With Favorite Songs   Scholastic Teaching Resources   **page 47**

Down by the Bay

Down by the Bay

Down by the bay
where the watermelons grow,
back to my home
I dare not go.
For if I do,
my mother will say,
"Did you ever see a cat
wearing a hat
down by the bay?"

Additional Verses:

Did you ever see...
    a snake baking a cake . . . ?
    a moose kissing a goose . . . ?
    a duck driving a truck . . . ?
    a pig wearing a wig . . . ?
    a mouse building a house . . . ?

Develop Oral Language

Introduce the Song

Copy enough picture cards (pages 50–51) so that you have one for each student. Color and cut apart the cards. Review the names for the pictures and then hand them out to students. Ask students to hold up their picture when they hear their word sung.

Sing It Again

- Work with children to create a motion for each verb (*wearing, baking,* and so on). Sing the song together, doing the motion for each verse.

- As you sing each verse, leave out the second word in the rhyming pair to create an oral cloze—for example, "Did you ever see a cat wearing a ____?" Invite students to fill in the missing words.

Build Phonemic Awareness

- **Sound Discrimination**   Instead of using a rhyming pair of words in each verse, substitute two words that begin with the same sound—for example, "Did you ever see an elephant wearing an eggshell?" Ask students for suggestions and then sing each new verse together.

- **Oddity Task**   Copy and cut apart the picture cards. Display two pictures that rhyme and one that does not. Ask students to identify the nonrhyming word.

Attend to Print

Preparing the Pocket Chart

Write each line of the first verse on a sentence strip. For the last lines of the song, leave blanks as follows:

"Did you ever see a _____
_____ a _____
down by the bay?"

Cut the strips into individual words. Place the text in the pocket chart. Create word cards for each animal, verb, and noun (such as *cat, wearing, hat*).

Read Together

- Place an animal picture card in the first blank. Fill in the second blank with the corresponding verb word card. Leave the third blank empty. Hand out the remaining picture cards to students. When you read the text aloud, the student holding the card that rhymes with the animal places it in the third blank. Repeat with other animals.

- Choose two picture cards at random and place them in the pocket chart in the first and third blanks. Use any verb card you wish. Read the text aloud with children. Ask, "Do the words for these pictures rhyme?"

- Remove all the cards from the pocket chart. Place several picture cards in a column along the left-hand side of the chart. Place their matching word cards at the bottom of the chart. Challenge students to match the word cards to the pictures and place them side by side.

- Using a pointer or word frame, challenge students to identify the following high-frequency words in the text: *by, the, where, to, my, I, for, will, did, you, see*.

Write Together

- **Class Book**   Give each student a copy of the class book (page 52). Ask children to create an additional verse for the song. Remind them that they should fill in the first and third blanks with rhyming words and the second blank with an action word. Encourage them to illustrate the page to match the text. Add a cover and bind the pages together to create a class book.

- **Short Story**   Let children choose one of the "Did you ever see . . ." lines from the song and build a story around it. For example, "Once upon a time there was a duck who wanted to drive south instead of flying . . ." Have students write or dictate their stories and then illustrate them.

- **Word Family Mobiles**   Choose a rhyming pair from the song, such as *cat* and *hat*. Write each word on an index card. Work together with children to record other words in that same family on index cards, such as *mat* and *rat*. Punch holes in the bottom and top of each card and string them together, one on top of another. Hang them in the classroom to create a spelling resource for students. Create other word-family mobiles based on rhyming pairs from the song.

- **Mini-Book**   Give each child a copy of the mini-book (pages 53–54). Have them write their name on the cover. Read the text with them and help them fill in the blanks with rhyming words. Remind them to use the illustrations as clues. Encourage them to read their book with a classmate before bringing it home to share with families.

50

Picture Cards

Picture Cards

Did you ever see a _____

_____ing a _____?

Name _____

Teaching Reading & Writing With Favorite Songs   Scholastic Teaching Resources

Class Book

7

Did you ever see a pig

wearing a _____?

2

Down by the bay
where the watermelons grow,
back to my home
I dare not go.
For if I do,
my mother will say . . .

Did you ever see a mouse

building a _____?

8

Down by the Bay

Name _____

1

5

Did you ever see a moose

kissing a _____?

Did you ever see a snake

baking a _____?

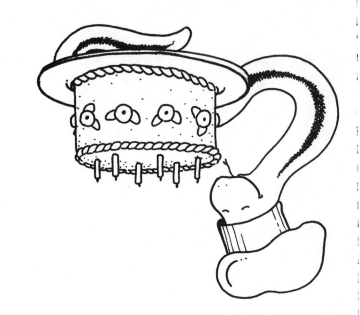

Did you ever see a duck

driving a _____?

Did you ever see a cat

wearing a _____?

Bingo

VOCABULARY

■ Pets' Names

Bingo

There was a farmer had a dog,
and Bingo was his name-o.
B-I-N-G-O!
B-I-N-G-O!
B-I-N-G-O!
And Bingo was his name-o!

Additional Verses:
(Clap) I-N-G-O
(Clap) (Clap) N-G-O
(Clap) (Clap) (Clap) G-O
(Clap) (Clap) (Clap) (Clap) O
(Clap) (Clap) (Clap) (Clap) (Clap)

Develop Oral Language

Introduce the Song

Write each letter in *Bingo* on an index card, filling each card with a large letter. Place these in a row on the chalkboard ledge or in a pocket chart. When you are teaching children the additional verses, turn over the appropriate index cards to show that children should clap instead of singing that letter.

Sing It Again

• Work together with students to think of other names for Bingo that have five letters in them, such as Mabel or Rover. Sing the song using the new names.

• Make enlarged copies of the cards on page 57. Cut apart the cards and display them as you are teaching children the song. Show children how to fingerspell the letters in Bingo's name. Sing the song again and let students sign the letters as they sing them:

B   I   N   G   O

Build Phonemic Awareness

• **Phonemic Manipulation** Ask children to create new names for Bingo by substituting different first letters (*Tingo, Dingo, Ringo,* and so on).

• **Sound Recognition** Use this adaptation of the song to review short vowel sounds:

There was a farmer had a vowel,
and short *a* was its name-o.
/a/, /a/, /a/, /a/, /a/!
/a/, /a/, /a/, /a/, /a/!
/a/, /a/, /a/, /a/, /a/!
And short *a* was its name-o!

55

Attend to Print

Preparing the Pocket Chart

Write each line of the first verse on a sentence strip. Cut the strips into individual word cards and place them in the pocket chart. Use 3- by 5-inch index cards to create other five-letter pet names (you'll need three of each).

Read Together

- Cover up the *B* in each spelled-out "B-I-N-G-O." Ask students to read the word without that letter (*INGO*). Continue to cover up other letters.

- Cut each spelled-out "B-I-N-G-O" into separate letters. Scramble them and challenge students to put the letters back in the correct order.

- Challenge students to find shorter words within the word *Bingo* (*bin, in, go*). Repeat with other pet names.

- Remove all the cards from the pocket chart. Choose any nine word cards and place them in a 3-by-3 grid formation. Challenge students to read three words horizontally, vertically, or diagonally. Each time a student reads three words successfully, he or she can call out, "Bingo!"

Write Together

- **Class Book**   Give each student a copy of the class book (page 58). Instruct them to fill in the first blank with any noun that refers to a person (*girl, boy, firefighter, teacher,* and so on). Have them think of a type of pet and fill in the second blank with the pet's name. Invite them to illustrate the page to match the text. Add a cover and bind the pages together to create a class book.

- **New Verses**   Work together with students to write additional verses for the song based on other farm animals. For example:

  > There was a farmer had a pig,
  > and Pinky was his name-o.
  > P-I-N-K-Y!
  > P-I-N-K-Y!
  > P-I-N-K-Y!
  > And Pinky was his name-o!

- **Mini-Book**   Give each child a copy of the mini-book (page 59). Have students write their name on the cover. Read the text with them and help them fill in the blanks with missing letters on page 3 and Bingo's name on page 4. Encourage them to read their book with a classmate before bringing it home.

B

I

N

G

O

Picture Cards

There was a _____ had a pet

and _____ was his name-o!

Name _____

Teaching Reading & Writing With Favorite Songs Scholastic Teaching Resources

3

B-I-———-G-O!

B-———-N-G-O!

-I-N-G-O!

2

There was a farmer had a dog,
and Bingo was his name-o.

And _____
was his name-o!

4

BINGO

BINGO

Name _____

1

The Bear Went Over the Mountain

The Bear Went Over the Mountain

The bear went over the mountain,
the bear went over the mountain,
the bear went over the mountain,
to see what he could see.

To see what he could see,
to see what he could see.

The other side of the mountain,
the other side of the mountain,
the other side of the mountain,
was all that he could see.

Was all that he could see,
was all that he could see.
The other side of the mountain
was all that he could see!

Develop Oral Language

Introduce the Song

Create a mountain to use as a prop while singing the song. Push two chairs back to back. Stack textbooks on each seat. Cover the chairs with a brown sheet, tablecloth, or blanket. As you sing, move a bear puppet over the "mountain." (Photocopy, color, and cut out the puppet on page 62. Glue a craft stick onto the back.) Substitute other directional words (*under, up, down,* and *around*) and let children take turns moving the puppet accordingly as the class sings.

Sing It Again

- Ask each child to bring in a stuffed animal. Sing the song and substitute the animal names as children take turns moving their animals over the mountain.

- Ask children what sense is mentioned in the song. (*sight*) Can they name the other senses? Sing the song again, substituting *hear, feel, taste,* and *smell* for *see*—for example, ". . . to hear what he could hear."

Build Phonemic Awareness

- **Rhyme**   Gather or draw pictures of objects whose names rhyme with *bear* (*chair, hare, mare, pear, square*) and place them in a box at the foot of the mountain (see Introduce the Song). Also include pictures or drawings of objects whose names do not rhyme. Let children take turns selecting a picture. If the name of the picture rhymes with *bear*, have the student move the picture over the mountain. Explain that nonrhyming words should stay where they are.

- **Oral Blending** Use the bear puppet (See Introduce the Song) to help children blend words. Choose a word from the song. Have the puppet "say" the word in parts, such as /w/ /e/ /n/ /t/. Ask children to blend the parts together and name the word. Repeat with other words.

Attend to Print

Preparing the Pocket Chart

Write the following on sentence strips:

> The bear went over the mountain
> to see what he could see.
> The other side of the mountain
> was all that he could see.

Cut apart the sentence strips into individual words. Place the text in the pocket chart. Copy, color, and cut apart the picture cards (page 62) and add these to the pocket chart.

Read Together

- Point to a word. Ask children to name the word that is "below the word," "two words to the left of the word," and so on. Repeat using other directional words such as *right, beside,* or *above.*

- Choose a mystery word from the text. Give children clues that incorporate some directional words. For example, "I'm thinking of a word that is below the word *went* and to the right of the word *see.*" Challenge students to identify the word.

Write Together

- **Class Book** Give each student a copy of the class book (page 63). Ask them to use their imaginations to think of what the bear might have seen on the other side of the mountain. Invite them to illustrate the page to match the text. Add a cover and bind the pages together to create a class book.

- **Labels** Cut out a large mountain from brown craft paper. Staple it to a bulletin board. Work together with children to label the mountain with directional words such as *left, right, beside, top, bottom, above, below,* and *inside.* (For *inside,* create a flap in the mountain and place the word *inside* underneath the flap.) Attach the bear puppet to a spot on the mountain and have children use directional words to name his location—for example, "He is to the left of the mountain." Continue to move the bear to different locations.

- **Mini-Book** Give each child a copy of the mini-book (page 64). Have them write their name on the cover. Read the book with them and help them fill in the blanks with directional words to match the illustrations (page 2: *up* or *over;* page 3: *down;* page 4: *through*). Encourage students to read their book with a classmate before bringing it home to share with families.

Picture Cards and Puppet

The bear went over the mountain to see what he could see.

He saw _____

Name _____

The bear went
_____ the mountain
to see what he could see.

The bear went
_____ the mountain
to see what he could see.

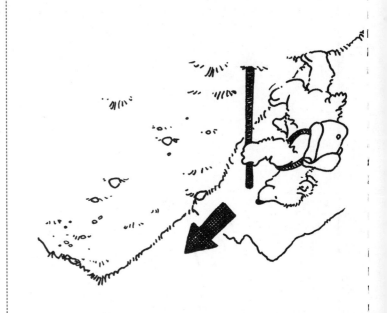

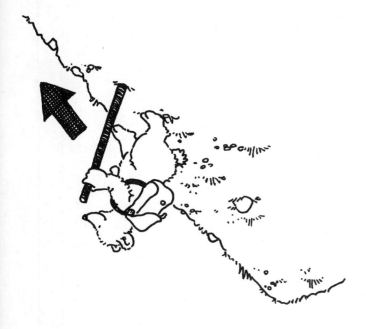

The bear went
_____ the mountain
to see what he could see.

The Bear Went Over the Mountain

Name _____